Mary McLeod Bethune

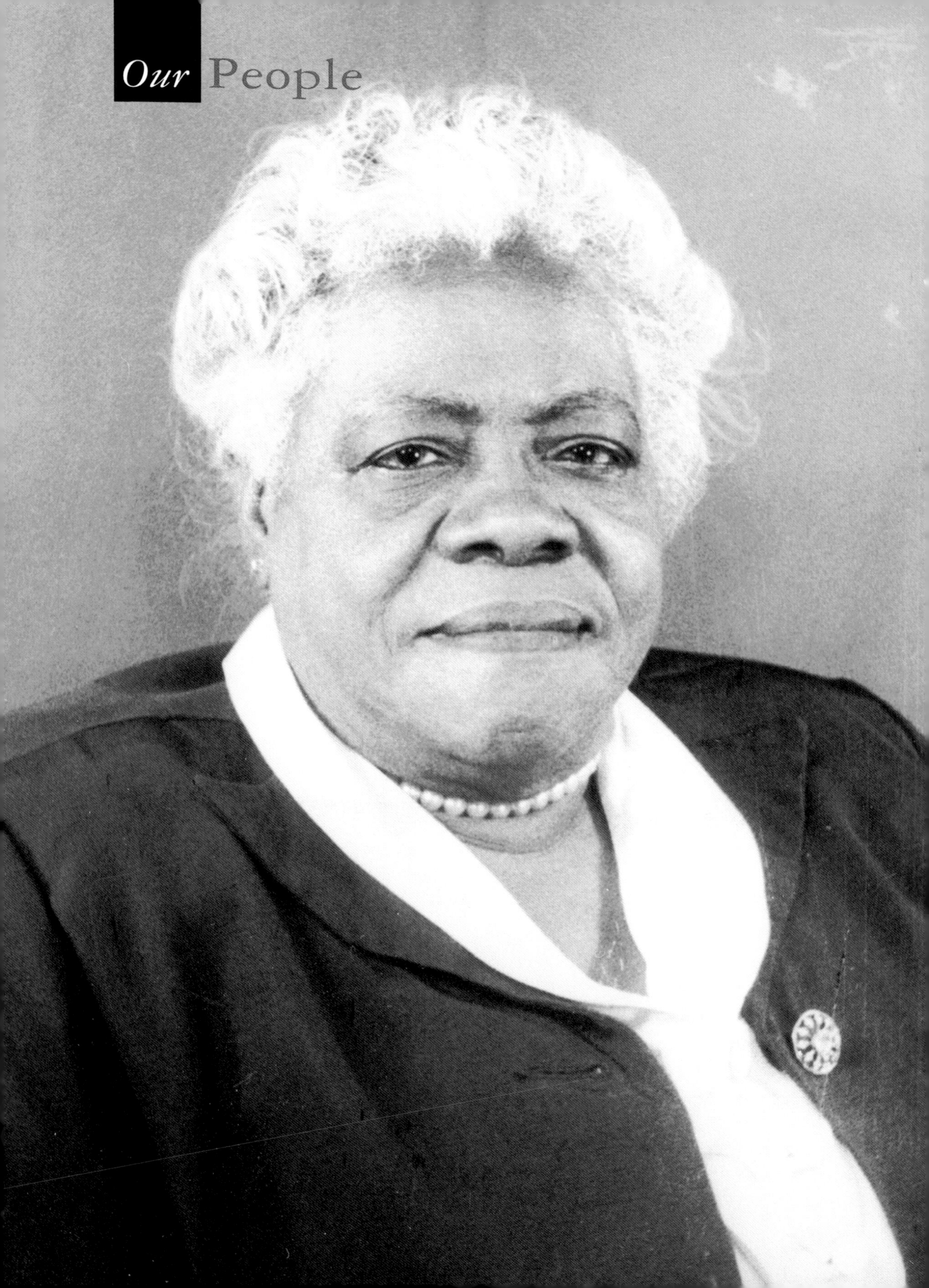

SPIRIT
of America®

MARY MCLEOD *Bethune*

AFRICAN-AMERICAN EDUCATOR

By Barbara A. Somervill

Content Adviser: Robert Hall, Museum Educator, Washington, D.C.

The Child's World®
Chanhassen, Minnesota

6

MARY MCLEOD *Bethune*

Published in the United States of America by The Child's World®
PO Box 326 • Chanhassen, MN 55317-0326 • 800-599-READ • www.childsworld.com

Acknowledgments
The Child's World®: Mary Berendes, Publishing Director

Editorial Directions, Inc.: E. Russell Primm, Editorial Director; Pam Rosenberg, Line Editor; Elizabeth K. Martin, Assistant Editor; Olivia Nellums, Editorial Assistant; Susan Hindman, Copy Editor; Susan Ashley, Halley Gatenby, Proofreaders; Jean Cotterell, Kevin Cunningham, Peter Garnham, Fact Checkers; Tim Griffin/IndexServ, Indexer; Dawn Friedman, Photo Researcher; Linda S. Koutris, Photo Selector

Photo
Cover: Estate of Carl Van Vechten and Beinecke Rare Book & Manuscript Library, Yale University; AP/Wide World Photos: 17 top, 23 top; Estate of Carl Van Vechten and Beinecke Rare Book & Manuscript Library, Yale University: 2; courtesy of Bethune-Cookman College Archives: 18; Corbis: 11 bottom, 16; Bettmann/Corbis: 17 bottom, 20, 21, 22: Hulton Archive/Getty Images: 8, 19, 23 bottom; Gordon Parks/Library of Congress: 10, 25, 26; Carl Mydans/Library of Congress: 11 top; Moody Bible Institute, Chicago, IL: 9; courtesy of Prints & Photographs, Moorland-Spingarn Research Center, Howard University: 14; Photographic Collection, Florida State Archives: 6, 7, 12, 13, 27, 28; The Procter & Gamble Company: 15.

Registration
The Child's World®, Spirit of America®, and their associated logos are the sole property and registered trademarks of The Child's World®.

Library of Congress Cataloging-in-Publication Data
Somervill, Barbara A.
  Mary McLeod Bethune : African-American educator / by Barbara A. Somervill.
    p. cm. — (Our people)
"Spirit of America."
Contents: The drums of Africa—Legacy of learning—A life of service—A diamond in the rough.
  ISBN 1-59296-008-1 (Library Bound : alk. paper)
 1. Bethune, Mary McLeod, 1875–1955—Juvenile literature. 2. African American women political activists—Biography—Juvenile literature. 3. African American women educators—Biography—Juvenile literature. 4. African American women social reformers—Biography—Juvenile literature. 5. African Americans—Biography—Juvenile literature. 6. African Americans—Civil rights—History—20th century—Juvenile literature. [1. Bethune, Mary McLeod, 1875–1955. 2. Teachers. 3. African Americans—Biography. 4. Women—Biography.] I. Title. II. Series.
E185.97.B34S67 2004
 370'.92—dc21   2003004257

Contents

Chapter ONE

The Drums of Africa

Mary McLeod Bethune spent her life working to ensure that good educational opportunities were available to African-Americans.

MARY MCLEOD BETHUNE SAID: "FOR I AM my mother's daughter, and the drums of Africa still beat in my heart. They will not let me rest while there is a single Negro boy or girl without a chance to prove his worth." Bethune believed that education could provide better lives for African-Americans. She worked throughout her life to fulfill this belief.

Mary Jane McLeod was born July 10, 1875, in Mayesville, South Carolina. Mary was the 15th of 17 children. Her parents, Samuel and Patsy McIntosh McLeod, had been enslaved. Many of the McLeod children had also been enslaved.

When the McLeods were freed from slavery after the Civil War, they were eventually able to buy a 5-acre (2-hectare) farm called the Homestead. Patsy continued to work for her former masters to earn extra money. Samuel and the children plowed and planted their land with cotton. Young Mary grew up working the fields. She once claimed that she could pick 250 pounds (114 kilograms) of cotton a day.

Samuel and Patsy McLeod were Mary McLeod Bethune's parents.

When Mary was 10, Trinity Presbyterian Mission School opened near the farm. The McLeods could only afford to have one child go to school. Patsy decided that Mary would be the one. Mary rose early each day and did her farm chores. Then, she walked 5 miles (8 kilometers) to school. More than anything, she wanted to learn. Her demanding schedule of farm chores and schoolwork helped young Mary to understand the importance of hard work in achieving success.

This small, wooden building was a school for African-Americans in Savannah, Georgia.

Mary's teacher, Emma Wilson, arranged for her to attend Scotia Seminary in Concord, North Carolina. Scotia followed the head-heart-hand method of education. Studying English, Latin, math, science, social studies, and religion taught the "head." Educating the "heart" meant Bible study and serving the community. Training for jobs that included cooking, cleaning, sewing, and gardening took care of the "hand" learning. Mary graduated from Scotia in 1894.

From Scotia, Mary attended the Moody Bible Institute in Chicago. She hoped to become a **missionary.** However, there were no openings for African-American missionaries to Africa. Disappointed, Mary returned to the South to teach. She knew that African-

Americans in the South needed a good education as much as people in Africa. She decided, "My life work lay not in Africa in my own country."

In Augusta, Georgia, Mary taught at the Haines Institute from 1896 to 1897. She also organized the Mission Sabbath School. These Sunday classes served 275 of Augusta's poorest children.

Mary McLeod Bethune attended the Moody Bible Institute in Chicago, Illinois, in 1865.

Interesting Fact

▶ Albert McLeod
Bethune died in
1989. He lived to
be 90 years old
and spent most of
his life in Daytona
Beach, Florida.

*Mary McLeod Bethune
and her son, Albert
McLeod Bethune*

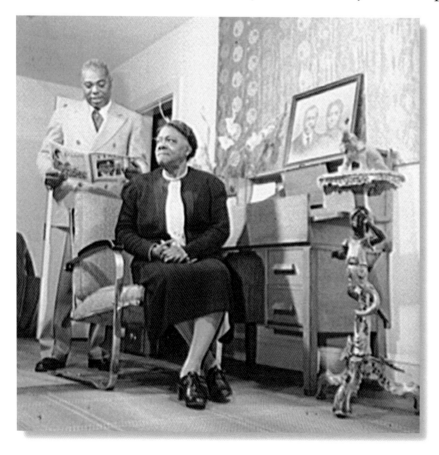

Mary moved from Augusta to Sumter, South Carolina, to teach at the Kendall Institute. There, she met and married Albertus Bethune in 1898. The following year, the Bethunes had a son, Albert McLeod Bethune. The marriage did not last long, however. Within a few years, Mary and Albertus went their separate ways.

A Florida minister encouraged Mary to move to Palatka, Florida. There, she cared for young Albert and taught school. She also did charity work. Mary visited prisoners in the local jails and workers at the sawmills. She stayed in Palatka for five years. Then, Mary learned that Daytona Beach, Florida, was a growing area in need of her skills. Daytona Beach would become Mary's permanent home.

AFTER THE CIVIL WAR (1861–1865), AFRICAN-American slaves were freed. Unfortunately, most had no skills for earning a living. Few freed slaves could read, write, or do math. The one job they knew was growing cotton. "King Cotton" ruled the South. But freed slaves had no money to buy land.

White landowners needed people to work their fields. They started sharecropping. Landowners would loan African-Americans land, tools, seed, and food. Black sharecroppers would pay back landowners with cotton after the fall harvest. A contract said how much the sharecropper would pay the landowner. Because most sharecroppers could not read, they were often cheated.

Some freed slaves were able to buy small farms like the McLeods did. They, too, were cheated in local markets and when their cotton was sold. Land-owners and cotton buyers sometimes claimed that the cotton weighed less than its real weight. An African-American farmer might get paid for 300 pounds (136 kg) when the cotton really weighed 400 pounds (182 kg).

Sharecroppers and free black farmers bought food and seed at the local stores. Many white storeowners claimed that the sharecroppers and farmers bought more than they did and charged them more money. This wasn't true, and many African-Americans knew they were being cheated. But without reading skills, they could not prove it.

Chapter Two

Legacy of Learning

WITH ONLY $1.50 IN HER POCKET, MARY McLeod Bethune began the Daytona Educational and Industrial Institute in 1904. She taught African-American girls in the head-heart-hand style of education. Her goal was to prepare them to be homemakers, workers, and good **citizens.**

Mary McLeod Bethune and a group of students from the Daytona Educational and Industrial Institute

Classes included reading, writing, and mathematics, as well as Bible study. In addition to regular school subjects, Bethune planned a farm. The farm would feed her students and teachers. It would produce sugarcane syrup, melons, pumpkins, tomatoes, and a variety of peas and beans. Students learned to sew, cook, and clean. They also read their Bibles and worked in the community.

In addition to regular school subjects, Mary McLeod Bethune's students were also taught how to cook, sew, and clean.

Mary McLeod Bethune spoke out for the rights of African-Americans.

Bethune's school opened with five students. Each paid 50 cents a week. For children whose families could not afford the 50 cents, school was free. Bethune never refused to teach a child because the parents could not pay. Money was important, but education came first. Bethune's first students sat on crates. They wrote with bits of wood dipped in elderberry juice.

In 1907, the Daytona Institute moved to a larger building. The school continued to grow. By 1910, 106 students attended the school and 76 actually lived on **campus.** Bethune dreamed of expanding the school. She wanted to add a kindergarten. She wanted to start a training college that taught the trades of rug weaving and broom making, to provide new skills for earning a living. Bethune also wanted to have nurses' training and a hospital for African-Americans.

The problem, as always, was money. During the winter, Daytona Beach filled with rich northerners seeking warmer weather. Bethune marched her students into fancy hotels to sing gospel songs. She spoke to the hotel guests about her school and asked for money. Her biggest supporters included James Gamble of the Procter & Gamble company and Thomas White of White Sewing Machines.

James N. Gamble, son of the founder of the Procter & Gamble Company, was one of Bethune's biggest supporters.

The Daytona Institute added a high school. In the early 1920s, few African-Americans attended high school and even fewer graduated. In 1920, Bethune's high school had 72 students. Seven graduated. The rest of Florida had only 505 African-American high school students total. Eighteen of them graduated.

In 1923, Bethune's school joined with the Cookman Institute in Jacksonville, Florida. The new school became Bethune-Cookman College and was established in Daytona Beach.

Interesting Fact

▶ Bethune used extra money she made selling insurance to pay off the "Homestead" in Mayesville, South Carolina. She also purchased a modern home for her parents to live in.

Bethune's dream of providing African-American boys and girls with a strong education was now a reality. The National Association for the Advancement of Colored People (NAACP) awarded Bethune the Spingarn Medal for her work in education. The Spingarn Medal is given each year to an African-American who has done outstanding work.

Mary McLeod Bethune in her office at Bethune-Cookman College

16

POWERFUL SOUTHERNERS PASSED LAWS TO KEEP African-Americans **segregated** from whites. African-Americans attended all-black schools. They could not eat in white restaurants or shop in white stores. They used "colored" restrooms and water fountains. They could only live in certain sections of towns. These laws were called Jim Crow laws. Jim Crow was a white stage actor who put on **blackface** and made fun of African-Americans.

Many African-Americans thought these laws were unfair. Homer Plessy decided to test the laws. Plessy had been arrested in New Orleans, Louisiana, for riding in a "whites only" railroad car. He took his case—*Plessy v. Ferguson*— to the United States Supreme Court. In 1896, the Court decided that Jim Crow laws were fair. States could provide "separate but equal" schools, restrooms, hospitals, and other places for blacks and whites.

African-American schools suffered badly. Whites attended large schools with 20 to 30 students per class. White schools had books for every student and plenty of supplies. Many African-American students attended small, one-room schools. They suffered through winter with no heat. An African-American teacher often taught 100 or more students. Sometimes 10 children had to share one book. Schools were "separate," but were not "equal."

In 1954, Linda Brown's parents won a lawsuit against the school board of Topeka, Kansas, over Linda's schooling. In *Brown v. Board of Education of Topeka,* the Supreme Court ruled that separate was not equal. The Court ordered states to desegregate their schools. African-American children were finally able to go to the same schools as white children.

Chapter THREE

A Life of Service

MARY McLEOD BETHUNE BELIEVED IN community service. In Daytona Beach, she supported **temperance** and **woman suffrage.** In 1917, she became president of the Florida Federation of Colored Women. This group supported charities and women's causes throughout the state. Seven years later, the National Association of Colored Women chose Bethune as its president. This was the highest office open to an African-American woman in the 1920s.

Mary McLeod Bethune was a member of many organizations that supported equal rights for African-Americans. She is pictured here with members of the National Council of Negro Women.

Bethune knew that voting meant power for African-Americans. In Florida, blacks had to pass a reading and writing test in order to vote. Blacks also had to pay a voting, or poll, tax. Bethune began teaching reading and writing to adults at night. She went from door-to-door on her bicycle collecting money to pay the poll tax. In 1920, she led 100 African-Americans to the polling place to vote for the first time.

By the mid-1920s, Bethune saw financial trouble ahead. Florida had enjoyed a land

Like the women in this parade, Mary McLeod Bethune supported suffrage for women.

Interesting Fact

▸ Mary McLeod Bethune had one son, Albert McLeod Bethune, and one grandson, Albert McLeod Bethune, Jr. She had 11 great-grandchildren.

boom. People had to pay very high prices to own land. Then, in 1925, the land boom went bust. During the next five years, the state suffered two major hurricanes. By the time the New York Stock Exchange crashed in 1929, Florida was already struggling. The **Great Depression** soon gripped the country. Bethune described that time as "the most severe test of our lives." She wanted to help African-Americans survive these hard economic times.

Bethune's deeds brought her national attention. Presidents Calvin Coolidge and Herbert Hoover asked her to attend meetings about child welfare. In 1932, Bethune was named one of the 50 greatest American women in a newspaper article. Her greatest fame, however, came from her friendship with President Franklin D. Roosevelt and First Lady Eleanor Roosevelt.

Many people lost their homes and lived in shantytowns, like this one in Seattle, Washington, during the Great Depression.

In 1935, Bethune created the National Council of Negro Women (NCNW). She served as the group's leader until 1949. The NCNW became involved in events that affected the nation. These events included public education, jobs, better health, and housing for African-American women and children.

Bethune advised Roosevelt about issues that concerned African-Americans. She saw that many young people had lost hope. They could not get jobs or improve their lives. In 1936, she became director of the Division of Negro Affairs of the National Youth

Mary McLeod Bethune was a friend and adviser to Eleanor Roosevelt (center).

Interesting Fact

Mary McLeod Bethune's hobbies included collecting photos of men and women whose accomplishments were outstanding. She also collected miniature elephants and the walking canes of famous men.

21

Mary McLeod Bethune at a meeting to discuss training African-American women to be officers in the Women's Army Auxiliary Corps.

Administration (NYA). Bethune provided job training for African-Americans through the NYA. Over the years, nearly five million youths found jobs.

World War II (1939–1945) ended the Great Depression. Suddenly, there were jobs for everyone. Manufacturing plants made goods to support the war. Men joined the military, while women worked in factories.

Bethune saw that African-Americans did not have an equal chance for success in the military. She asked the U.S. War Department to name African-American women as officers in the Women's Army Auxiliary Corps. She pushed for African-Americans to become pilots and officers in the military. A true patriot, Bethune supported the government's war effort. She encouraged other African-Americans to do the same.

IN OCTOBER 1929, THE NEW YORK STOCK Exchange (left) crashed. This economic disaster started the Great Depression (1929–1939). Millions of people suffered as the economy sank deeper into trouble.

Here's how the stock market works. Companies sell parts of their businesses, called shares of stock, at the stock exchange. A person, bank, or other company might buy 100 shares of XYZ Company at $10 per share. If XYZ does well, the share value might rise to $15 per share. Then the shareholder would have a $500 profit.

If XYZ does poorly, the shares lose their value. The 100 shares that were worth $1,000 originally might later be worth only $500. When the stock market crashed, the shares of all companies lost value. Shares of stock became worthless. Shareholders lost all the money they had invested.

Some people put their money in bank accounts. To make more money, banks bought shares of stock. When the stock market crashed, banks lost all their money. The banks could not pay back their account holders. Banks closed, too.

During the Depression, people couldn't afford to buy products, like cars or new clothes. Companies making products couldn't sell them. They had to stop manufacturing products and close their factories. Millions of workers lost their jobs. Many lost their homes. Those who suffered the most were the poor. They had little to start with and ended up with nothing.

A Diamond in the Rough

WHEN WORLD WAR II ENDED IN 1945, MARY McLeod Bethune was 70 years old. Yet her work did not end. Bethune represented the United States at meetings in San Francisco to organize the United Nations. There, she met many people of her race from Africa and Asia. Bethune supported their desire for freedom. However, she did not see much progress coming from all the discussions. She said, "San Francisco is not building the promised land of brotherhood and security and opportunity and peace. It is building a bridge to get there by. We still have a long way to go."

Bethune received a number of honors from other countries. In 1949, she went to Haiti to celebrate the 1949 Haitian Exposition. She was awarded the Medal of Honor and Merit.

It was Haiti's highest honor. That same year, she represented the United States when Liberia's President William Tubman took his second oath of office. It was her first trip to Africa. She had once dreamed of

Mary McLeod Bethune reads her Bible. She once dreamed of becoming a missionary in Africa.

being an African missionary. Now, she was there as the official representative of the United States. She received Liberia's most valued award, naming her Commander of the Order of the Star of Africa.

In 1953, she set up the Mary McLeod Bethune Foundation. The foundation oversees a library of Bethune's papers, speeches, and letters from throughout her life. There are many diaries, scrapbooks, and files from her work. The foundation holds the largest

Mary McLeod Bethune's home, located next to Bethune-Cookman College

Interesting Fact

▶ Mary McLeod Bethune made sure that six African-American colleges took part in the Civilian Pilot Training Program when World War II began. Her efforts opened the door to black pilots in the military.

collection of Bethune works in the world. It is located in her former home next to Bethune-Cookman College. Bethune hoped her foundation would inspire young people. She said, "I want this to always be a kind of a sacred place—a place to awaken people and to have them realize that this is something in the world they can do."

Bethune died of a heart attack on May 18, 1955. She was buried on the grounds of her beloved Bethune-Cookman College. Here is her last will and testament:

"I leave you love.… I leave you hope.… I leave you thirst for education.… I leave you a respect for the uses of power.…I leave you faith.…I leave you racial dignity.…"

Bethune-Cookman College continues to educate students from 35 countries. It is the sixth largest college in the United Negro College Fund group. Bethune-Cookman graduates work as teachers, nurses, writers, and social workers. They follow Mary McLeod Bethune's view that education creates opportunity for success.

Bethune received many honors for her efforts in public service, education, and race relations. In 1974, a statue of Bethune was placed in a park near the Capitol. It stands 17 feet (5.2 m) tall. This was the first statue in Washington, D.C., that represented either a woman or an

This statue of Mary McLeod Bethune is located in Washington, D.C.

Interesting Fact

▸ Today, over 2,700 full-time students attend Bethune-Cookman College.

Mary McLeod Bethune is remembered as a great American and an inspiration to many.

African-American. A year later, her home in Daytona Beach, Florida, became a National Historic Landmark. A postage stamp with her portrait was issued by the U.S. Postal Service. She is also in the Florida and South Carolina state halls of fame. She is considered by many people to have been one of the most productive and effective African-Americans in public life. The *Washington Afro-American* newspaper described Bethune as "a great American and a world citizen."

Throughout her life, Bethune found new ways for African-Americans to succeed. She believed that people should "invest in the human soul. Who knows, it might be a diamond in the rough." In many ways, that statement describes Bethune. The daughter of freed slaves, she was born poor and rose above it. She was, herself, a diamond in the rough who went on to become a leader and an inspiration to many.

Time LINE

1875   1904   1953

1875   Mary Jane McLeod is born in Mayesville, South Carolina, the 15th of 17 children.

1894   McLeod graduates from Scotia Seminary, Concord, North Carolina.

1896–1897   McLeod teaches at Haines Institute, Augusta, Georgia.

1898   Albertus Bethune marries Mary Jane McLeod.

1899   Albert McLeod Bethune is born to Albertus and Mary.

1904   Mary McLeod Bethune opens the Daytona Educational and Industrial Institute with five students and $1.50 in cash.

1923   Daytona Institute merges with Cookman Institute to become Bethune-Cookman College. Bethune wins the NAACP Spingarn Medal in honor of her work in education.

1924   Bethune is elected president of the National Association of Colored Women.

1935   Bethune forms the National Council of Negro Women.

1936   Bethune is named director of the Division of Negro Affairs of the National Youth Administration (NYA), the first African-American woman to receive a major appointment from the federal government.

1940   NAACP (National Association for the Advancement of Colored People) chooses Bethune as vice president.

1945   Bethune represents the United States in San Francisco at the organization of the United Nations.

1949   Haiti honors Bethune with the Medal of Honor and Merit, the country's highest award. Bethune represents the United States at the inauguration of President William Tubman of Liberia.

1955   Mary McLeod Bethune dies of a heart attack and is buried on the campus of her beloved Bethune-Cookman College.

blackface (BLAK-fayss)
Blackface is makeup applied to a white performer playing a black person in a show. Jim Crow was a white stage actor who put on blackface and made fun of African-Americans.

campus (KAM-puhss)
A campus is the land and the buildings that make up a school. Mary McLeod Bethune is buried on the campus of Bethune-Cookman College.

citizens (SIT-I-zuhns)
Citizens are the people who are born in or have the right to live in a particular country. Mary McLeod Bethune expected the young people she educated to become good citizens of the United States.

Great Depression (GRAYT di-PRESH-uhn)
The Great Depression was a time in which many banks and other businesses failed and millions of people were out of work. Mary McLeod Bethune wanted to help African-Americans cope with the hard economic times brought about by the Great Depression.

missionary (MISH-uh-ner-ee)
A missionary is someone sent by a religious group into a region to teach about their faith and do other good works. Mary McLeod Bethune hoped to become a missionary.

segregated (SEG-ruh-gay-ted)
The practice of keeping races separate in public and private facilities is known as segregation. African-Americans in the South were segregated even in travel and had to ride in "colored" railroad trains.

temperance (TEM-pur-uhns)
Temperance is moderation in all the things that you do. The people in the temperance movement wanted to limit or completely prohibit the sale of alcoholic beverages in the United States.

woman suffrage (WUM-uhn SUHF-rij)
Woman suffrage is the right of women to vote in public elections. Women in the United States did not gain woman suffrage in national elections until 1920.

For Further INFORMATION

Web Sites

Visit our homepage for lots of links about Mary McLeod Bethune:
http://www.childsworld.com/links.html

Note to Parents, Teachers, and Librarians:
We routinely verify our Web links to make sure they're safe,
active sites—so encourage your readers to check them out!

Books

Grant, Reg G. *The Great Depression.* Hauppauge, N.Y.: Barrons Educational Series, 2003.

Jones, Amy Robin. *Mary McLeod Bethune.* Chanhassen, Minn.: The Child's World, 2001.

Kelso, Richard. *Building a Dream: Mary Bethune's School.* Austin, Tex.: Raintree/Steck-Vaughan, 1996.

McKissack, Patricia, and Fred McKissack. *Mary McLeod Bethune.* Chicago: Childrens Press, 1992.

Places to Visit or Contact

Mary McLeod Bethune Council House National Historic Site
To tour the house that Bethune lived in when she was in Washington, D.C., which served as the first headquarters of the National Council of Negro Women
1318 Vermont Avenue, N.W.
Washington, DC 20005
202/673-2402

The Bethune Foundation
To write for more information about Mary McLeod Bethune and the college she founded
Bethune-Cookman College
640 Dr. Mary McLeod Bethune Boulevard
Daytona Beach, FL 32114
386/481-2000

Index

About the Author

BARBARA SOMERVILL IS THE AUTHOR OF MANY BOOKS FOR CHILDREN. She loves learning and sees every writing project as a chance to learn new information or gain a new understanding. Ms. Somervill grew up in New York State, but has also lived in Toronto, Canada; Canberra, Australia; California; and South Carolina. She currently lives with her husband in Simpsonville, South Carolina.